Dear ....

love
from ....